Seductive Secrets

Roger Rickard

Published by Roger Rickard, 2023.

SEDUCTIVE SECRETS

First edition. November 30, 2023.

Copyright © 2023 Roger Rickard.

ISBN: 979-8223744436

Written by Roger Rickard.

Table of Contents

This Book is dedicated to all the men out there who, maybe at some stage of their lives, have been reluctant, or unable to, confidently approach women with a view to establishing a relationship.

May they all feel happier and gain confidence that may have eluded them.

Author's important note

This book is intended for Western structured, or Christian, and other similar value-based societies, as they're commonly referred to.

The information and techniques contained in this book can only be applied to a society or culture where the laws dictate that there is an equal balance of communication and social interaction, legally, for both men and women.

For societies or cultures where the respective laws prevent the equal rights for men and women, the teachings and techniques given in this book are simply not applicable.

That said, if men from unequal rights, religions, or cultures learn and try these techniques, and experiment with Western Cultured women, they can be assured that they will fail in their attempts and objectives.

Why?

The reasons are that normal women (especially normally balanced Western Cultured women) have in-built and intuitive systems to detect and to naturally reject false, negative, abnormal, and unnatural advances from such alien cultured men.

Be warned - such men will invariably suffer detrimental self-inflicted consequences from their own arrogant or ego-based actions, from such women that they try to seduce.

This issue is further explained in more detail in one of the chapters.

The laws of nature, with respect to the intuitive gifts given to women, which have been around for thousands of years, thankfully, prevail.

PREFACE

This book contains no-nonsense information and assistance intended for heterosexual relationships.

The information is mainly intended for single or separated men looking to form a relationship, but it also can be applied to men in a married or partnership wishing to improve or resurrect their relationships.

There is also information on help when living with women, once an intimate relationship has been formed.

How many books have been written on the well-worn subject of man/woman relationships?

Countless, covering all the various common topics and subjects that make up relationships.

The reader will invariably recognise similar themes and parallels in this book, with the techniques of courting women, together with the terminology used, in other available sources.

Perhaps different words or phrases are used, and some material many delve deeper into various parts of the processes discussed.

However, this book's main purpose is to explain the process of intimate relationship building and maintenance as simply as possible, covering the essential elements involved.

It is a relatively short guide that can probably be read in one sitting, though to learn and appreciate the techniques, parts of the book would need to be re-read, perhaps more than once, at the individual's discretion.

The history of man, through the ages has shown, that women have, in many cases, been the main problem that has confronted and confused men, sometimes stopping them from succeeding and fulfilling their ambitions.

The guidelines contained in this book provide ways for men to find women and consequently manage this confusion.

The information will be helpful for your relationship whether you are about to start contemplating marriage or a relationship or have had one for some time.

INTRODUCTION

__WHY__ the so-called confusion or problem?

Men and Women?

Mainly because men and women are made differently– that would be the simplest explanation.

Let's state the well-worn cliché:

"Women are from Venus and Men are from Mars".

Well not totally true, but in terms of emotional traits and other characteristics, the cliché does indeed have some strong merits.

We didn't design the blueprints of nature; or set the architectural structure of men's and women's minds tens of thousands of years ago.

Our different genders are what they are.

We are what we are.

To get on in this world we must accept it; bite the bullet, so to speak.

So, to be as happy as we can strive to be, we need to get on with life and play the game, to appreciate that courtship rules need to be learnt, if they haven't been acquired naturally.

Some men learn the game of life easily and quickly.

Some, if indeed most men, need to dutifully apply and learn the skills of the game, to be comfortable and confident around women.

Some men, for whatever reasons, never learn or recognise the game of life they're in, and never form intimate relationships with women.

SEDUCTIVE SECRETS

Some women also don't learn their part to play or appreciate the rules; some deliberately flout them to their detriment.

A man/woman relationship is the cornerstone or the building block of our (Western) society.

The husband/wife, or partnership, de-facto etc (it has various contemporary names), together with children which form the common family unit, is the basis of our communities and society in which we live. This historic social concept can also be applied to the very small proportion of the population that live in isolated regions where facilities of basic social communities may not be accessible.

And yet many people do not comprehend or realise the main basic attributes or characteristics of the man/woman relationship.

I detest to use the word understand, because no one ever has, or ever will, fully understand the reasons for relationships, and the involvement of relationships.

We can perhaps approach the truth, if that is the right phrase, but we'll never find it; the truth will always elude us.

We are left with some form of approximation.

There is a need to protect oneself from women; there are strong possibilities that women can destroy you, which can be interpreted in any way that you wish: mentally, emotionally, financially, and so forth.

A common example being that middle or elderly aged men need to have financial safety devices or legal instruments in place, if entering a new relationship, especially with younger women. Of course, the converse can also be true.

If a couple are of similar young age, so twenty years of age and each have no sizable assets, then obviously no financial security tools, or requirements are probably needed. What they gain or accumulate (if they ever do!) would be invariably fairly shared between them if the situation arises where their relationship ends.

The topics and sections form a thread of techniques that are honest and practical, involving tried and tested sensible ways for men to enable their lives to be easier when acquiring and living with the opposite gender – women.

This book is divided into three distinct parts:

The first part of this book deals with the art of finding and attaining a woman.

It would be fair to say that a fair proportion of men are not attuned to the custom of finding, courting, and winning a mate (a woman).

Some men do find this process comfortable and straight forward.

But most men do find it very awkward and uncomfortable, become disillusioned, and are confused with the whole process of courting women; probably over fifty percent of men have problems with communication.

The methods described are proven ways to approach, court, and win a woman's heart, essentially forming a relationship.

There are definite skills involved, and they're not all taught in schools!

For some men these skills come naturally – perhaps they are lucky?

For other men, they may not achieve the skills needed to relate to women, and either enter relationships against their natural will or maybe never secure a satisfying life with the opposite sex.

It's hoped that the techniques discussed will provide valuable assistance for

the men who are uncomfortable in this respect, and can learn, practice, and

apply these skills to gain fulfilment in life.

The second part of this book applies once one is in a secure relationship. Men's ambitions can often be thwarted by being in a relationship with a woman. Other realities of day-to-day life with women can also prevent men from fulfilling their deep desires.

I'm sure the information here will provide some assistance in the understanding of man and woman relationships to assist all parties to smooth over natural friction and conflicts that occur.

I trust it provides some alleviation of confusion and problems to help you get through life more comfortably.

In the context of this book, among other relevant issues, we are interested in the chemistry between men and women forming a heterosexual relationship, and how this chemistry, providing it's there, may be exploited for mutual gain.

The third part of this book contains separate topics about various subjects that are in context with the art of relating to women and forming relationships.

The subjects have interesting information in their respective own rights; the reader may take or leave the information at their convenience.

Certain topics may seem to be repeated, and indeed, some aspects already covered in Parts 1 and 2 may seem unnecessarily repetitious.

However, the topics are presented in a different manner, which may aid the understanding, and will certainly provide reinforcement of the information.

Reading the book

To gain full benefit from the information of this book, it is suggested that any young novice commence reading and complete Part 1 in the order presented.

Various topics in Part 3 such as: *Dating; The Pick-Up; Tit-bits; and Technical Terms,* can be read at any time if desired for reinforcing the knowledge being learnt.

A man already established in a relationship may wish initially to read Part 2.

PART 1

The art of attracting and bedding a woman

How is it done?

What are the key elements?

Are there any shortcuts?

How long does it take?

Does it always have to be a certain specific played out courting process?

What's involved in courting?

Is it always the man who does the courting?

There are probably many other questions that men ask themselves when relating in the confused realm of women!

So, we'll begin with the basics and go on from there.

The two keys to indicate to a woman that *YOU* are interested in *HER* are simply:

TOUCH and *BODY LANGUAGE*

The process of bedding her involves stages of courting that, invariably, must be adhered to achieve your objective.

These stages involve techniques, actions, and then monitoring her feedback and behaviour.

It is a constant art of doing something and then observing her response.

It can involve a lot of patience and persistence.

If you're fortunate to be with a woman who has a good chemistry with you, then all this will come naturally; it will seem so straight forward with little or no effort.

A general outline of the whole courting process:

There are three objectives which will be explained in detail in their own way.

1. An initial, or *first objective* whereby you indicate to the woman your intentions, that is, you want to find out about her, hopefully be with her and get to know her – well!
2. The *second objective* is to build on the relationship that you started in the first objective; your behaviour and dialogue will be modified somewhat.
3. Lastly, *the third objective*, is an intensity of desire and attraction. Again, your dialogue and behavioural actions will be modified to achieve this.

Right, so without complicating things, throughout each of these three processes or *objectives*, there are about three or four subtle stages, within each objective, that need to be addressed and consciously be made aware of.

As you read through the book, familiarize yourself with the concepts of the objectives, and stages, so you're readily able to decode and ascertain at what particular point you are with women when courting them.

SEDUCTIVE SECRETS

Keep these *objectives*, and their relative stages, in the back of your mind, as you go through the processes, described below.

With a bit of practice, it will then become natural, without any difficulty, to understand where you are, and (most importantly) where she is, in the whole courting process.

You'll be able to establish the strength of your relationship with her, and where it's possibly going to go.

The stages are not numerically listed or specifically identified as such but can be interpreted within each *objective* procedure given.

These stages when courting women can be briefly described as:

- correctly and honestly showing your intentions to her

- earning her trust in you

- creating within her a desire for you

- (most importantly) assessing her responses to your actions; that is feedback, so you may decode her behaviour

These stages apply to each of the three *objectives*.

At first hand, the stages within each objective may seem confusing and complicated, but once you've learnt and established them in your sub-conscious mind, they will appear as a logic threaded process, and feel like obvious steps as you experience the courting process with women.

They follow a common, natural, and logical pattern.

OK then - on with it!

Objective 1

This is just a fun sort of phase where you show your intentions in a non-sexual way. Subtleness is the key here, to keep her guessing what you're going to do next.

When you first see a woman, to ensure that she can acknowledge that you "exist", you really have about three to five seconds to create an action to get her attention.

This is just a proven rule of thumb.

If you don't do anything at this point it will be very difficult, if not impossible, to claw back any attention from her later.

So, what do you do?

Little things, examples being:

   - create eye contact maybe for a couple of seconds then look away for a bit

   - a subtle sort of smile - some people refer to it as a smirk, which is not your normal full blown big grin "show all my teeth" smile, but a gentle, honest, naturally friendly little smirky type smile or grin

   - talk to her in a low but assertive tone

   - stand reasonably close, but just out of that: *"in my personal space two-feet (half a metre) range"*

SEDUCTIVE SECRETS

- keep a good posture with your shoulders back, chin up without showing any undue stress in your body

- present your body on some sort of angle to her, at this stage of the game; this indicates to her that you may just walk away - it shows her that you're not coming in a heavy sort of pretence - it keeps women guessing!

- if you're close enough, reach out and touch her – try to do this as soon as possible

Where do you touch her?

Wrists, elbows, maybe shoulders – any non-sensitive and non-sexual part of her body – just for a half a second; sort of like a symbolic handshake, or a friendly greeting.

Test her reaction.

Does she flinch or pull away, or stand her ground?

Talking

Some key points to note when talking.

Life, generally, is easier to get through when we all flirt with each other and keep a good sense of humour - so long as it's not overdone!

It's good to banter, or flirt, with everyone, not just women, but to our fellow men too, whether they be work mates or our best friends.

It's a good way to connect us all; we use appropriate topics or subjects depending on who we're being humorous or flirting with.

Women love flirting in a fun sort of way.

Depending on the environment, or situation where you meet a woman, you will find lots of ways to offer light, playful verbal banter and wit.

Don't try to amuse her, but be yourself, without being over polite.

What do you talk about?

Anything really.

A good idea is something that is in the immediate environment.

Wherever you are, at a show, an event, or at the beach, etc., there will be countless ideas to initiate a conversation.

Questions are best phrased that require more than a simple: Yes/No answer.

For example, don't ask: "Do you come to this park often?"

Phrase it like: "When was the last time you visited this park?"

Try and make smart and intuitive comments from observations, where you are with the woman.

Don't try and act as if you are somebody else.

Women can pick up on any false pretence at the blink of an eyelid!

BE Confident!

BE Yourself!

So, at this stage of the talking dialogue, we hopefully start to earn her trust and make some sort of emotional connection with her.

Share a bit about yourself, not your full life story, just little pieces.

SEDUCTIVE SECRETS

Keep part of your life and background a mystery to her.

Sparingly touch at appropriate times, maybe when you're both; laughing or nudging each other; maybe touch her wrist or arm in a light-hearted sort of way.

Be honest about yourself; don't feel ashamed about anything and feel free to admit to being vulnerable, if you are, about something you're both talking about.

Don't try to cover up or compensate.

You'll pick up her trust in you when she likes being around you; doesn't mind your occasional touch; jests and vibes in a friendly way and easily engages in free banter with you.

This is a good place to mention that you don't want her to think that you want her just as a friend.

Sure, intimate couples are of course close friends in the true sense, it's all part of a deep relationship, but we don't want her thinking that you're getting to know her solely to be good friends.

By the same token, we don't wish to come across as some sort of creep or pervert; that all we want is a good lay!

It's a kind of in-between zone that we need to constantly remind ourselves to be in, it's a bit of a balancing act.

Don't be afraid if you think you haven't got it quite right - no person gets things perfect all the time.

No mistakes mean no risk taking, and life involves taking (sensible) risks to achieve one's goals.

What are the signs to look out for that can indicate if you're maybe "over" or "under" the desired situation you're seeking?

The over friendly zone is when you're:

- not initiating conversations or actions

- overanalysing things

- trying to constantly appease her

- putting her on a pedestal

- not prepared to step out with small risks

Conversely, the overconfident creep will:

- take badly thought-out actions

- be aggressive

- come onto her too strong

- be constantly bantering

So, it's a balance of clearly showing your intentions, moving forward with self-confidence, and listening to what she's saying.

Only you can determine the balance from the situation with a particular woman. Every woman and situation will be different in its own way.

Don't be discouraged if you feel you've gone too far in one area – just back off a bit and carry on a different tact.

Nothing, and no one, is perfect all the time!

SEDUCTIVE SECRETS

From here, as we move through the stages, we'd be looking at trying to create a situation where she has a strong desire for you. We need to know that she's investing her time and energy into you (not you into her - but remember that you are anyway).

This stage of the game is important, as the outcome enables you to quite accurately see where your relationship with her is going, and how far it has come.

It's like releasing something and seeing if it will come back on its own accord.

The best time to try this is when say, for example, conversation is at a high.

You take away the mutual good feelings that are interacting between you and the woman by breaking your attention to her.

When you see that she is working to win your attention back, acknowledge it and be attentive again. She may have various ways of trying to re-invest in you;

you need to watch and observe them.

Examples to achieve this creation of desire for you could be by withholding your touch, if she initiates it – it will create an unpredictable sense from you.

Or, if she asks a sensitive question, respond with a joke rather than sharing more of your intimacy with her.

Don't be afraid to surprise her at times.

Pull her closer momentarily; or say something sexual very briefly before returning to a non-sexual conversation.

It's pushing the envelope at times to test the water – see how she responds, if she wants to come back to find out more about you.

We need to decode how the woman is reacting to your actions, things you say to her as you're building a relationship with her.

We need to be quite attentive to her responses.

For example, if she's "into you" she'll:

- return your touch

- maybe lean in or towards you

- be attentive and excited with regard to what you're saying

Conversely, if she doesn't have any high aspirations at this stage, she'll:

- back away

- provide just short, abrupt answers in conversations

- look around the room or surroundings more

Pulling back means she needs more from you.

She needs to feel a bit more comfortable with you before moving on.

So, you need to hold back a bit in terms of what you've been doing and continue to build up an emotional connection with her until she feels happy to move forward again.

Maybe this means using an amended style of flirting or bantering; perhaps behaving in a slightly more masculine way which brings out the femininity in woman.

Don't be discouraged if you receive no positive signals; it could be for a variety of reasons (it could be the wrong time of her menstrual cycle).

You'll know when she's ready to move on further by her behaviour, which of course, you have been looking for!

Positive cues from her would include:

- facing you

- arms open, perhaps hands on hips

- a good, positive posture

- maybe fixing her hair

- standing close to you when you talk

- focusing more attention on you, especially when there are other distractions

- playing with her clothes

- her flirting becomes more physical

- she's really interested in your answers to her questions

- playfully challenges you or teases you

- asks you to do something that she could do herself

- talks of future plans

- she has a strong response to what you think of her

- she strives for a good validation from you

Building a relationship isn't a predetermined hard and fast formula or procedure.

Don't try too hard; just concentrate on a steady natural flow.

It can take time and practice.

You can build confidence by practicing on your own.

Actors must do this to achieve their goals for theatre or films.

Practice saying your joke ideas; practice conversational threading – one idea to the next – thinking of the next thing to say.

Ideas come from the subject being talked about and immediate surroundings.

It's all part of the initial approach and starting conversations.

OK let's move on!

Objective 2

We lead on then to building the relationship.

Our actions are very similar to the first objective, but we behave in a more romantic and sensual manner.

We say things in a more sexual context and direction, as with our bantering, teasing and physical contact.

How?

By dropping words into the conversation like:

hard

stiff

soft

stroke

bedroom

thrust

rub

squeeze

bed

night time

hold

position

candle lights

smooth

These words on their own may mean nothing, but to a woman, if the words are slightly emphasised, when spoken, it triggers a subconscious mental state (maybe only momentarily) within them that they clearly will remember.

It will create a responsive sexual desire for them – and it was you that said it!

They are not direct sexual words, but when spoken in an acceptable context they create subtle sexual connections that women cannot ignore.

Women can't ignore or switch off these sounds or signs because it's built within their female primal architecture; it's all part of their natural breeding process.

You may find that you're talking about a sexual subject with her; admit that you find her sexy – tell her what is specifically sexy about her.

When we touch, again just in non-sensual places at this stage, we may linger the touch for a bit longer, like if we are alone in some place with the woman.

When you're both attentive to each other, maybe looking at her face, flick to various parts of it, mouth, eyes, etc.

This shows her that you want her, but you are controlled.

We'll build up her trust if we are not too timid, or conversely, aggressive.

SEDUCTIVE SECRETS

Emotionally connect with the conversation but add some serious pieces at times too.

Maybe you can bring back previous teases you shared; this creates a strong bond between you.

Achieving a situation where she desires you, again, can be from actions of not physically touching her when she would expect you to, then surprising her when she least expects it.

Again, try to be confident in everything you do.

Use "We" statements a lot in the conversations.

Women do need to see men's primal instincts igniting, as it, in turn, sparks their own primal instincts.

They have difficulty trying to spark their own instincts; us men invariably need to trigger it for them.

And if their primal instinct is done in a way they like, they'll respond positively and strongly to you.

Hence logical, or factual talk is not primal talk.

She wants a romantic adventure, like reading a stimulating novel – you need to give her that experience!

If she's into you, she'll love you for it.

In these stages, if she pulls back or away, for whatever reason which we don't know, as women's behaviour can be unpredictable at times, just stay cool and withdraw a bit with your actions and words.

Flick back to less sensual style like you were doing in *Objective 1*.

Then when you can decode her responses that she is ready to move forward, come back to this objective and stage to continue.

By now, it will be more obvious how to decode her behaviour and monitor the feedback from her.

Good positive signs from her would include:

- lingering physical contact with you.

- starring intently into your eyes.

- making efforts to get you alone.

- making the first move in some situations.

You could, of course, reciprocate these above examples anyway, just to see if she, in turn, will reciprocate to you.

She may say things in an indirect or subtle way just to protect herself from rejection, or to prevent feeling vulnerable.

It's a good idea to flick to touching her non-sensual areas at times too, like the back of her wrists or shoulders, rather than other sensual parts of her body that you may have been doing by now.

This is a form of "rejecting and coming back" which can reignite the woman's primal instincts.

Dialogue that may further ignite her instincts could include saying things, in parts of your conversation, like:

- "Curling up in bed with a book"

- "Drinking red wine by a cosy fire on a winter's night"

- "Cooking pasta with you over a hot stove"

Lots of those "sexy" words listed above work well too.

All these verbal sensual clues ignite her natural mental instincts, so slip these comments in where appropriate.

She'll desire you for saying them because it's highly likely you will have sparked her primal instincts!

Great – we're now getting to that juicy part of the relationship; in-between *Objectives 2 and 3* and about to launch into *Objective 3*.

Objective 3

We're heading towards the home stretch.

From here, we use more directness in our actions to build her desire for a lasting attraction to us.

We can consolidate our sexual directness by telling her what you want to do to her, perhaps in an indirect way, again using feedback awareness, to gauge her response.

This will provide you with clues that will assist you in what else to say to her, and how direct you think you could be, so she feels comfortable.

Perhaps tell her, "How she's driving you crazy".

Express what you'd like to do to her, in what you say.

By now, as we commence this *Objective 3* phase of the game, we no doubt will be kissing and touching around more sensual areas of her body.

Again, discretely pull back at times to create her desire to want more.

Use your intelligence and strategy to get her alone with you where YOU wish to go with her.

Women like to be TAKEN.

Make it your decision - not hers!

This really intoxicates them – they want you to lead them to exciting places, to environments they may not have been to before or experienced, something different to them.

Look for any opportunities to exploit that: "taking your woman somewhere".

SEDUCTIVE SECRETS

Imagine a hot summer's day, walking over remote green fields, conversing with her and touching in passionate ways; doing things together discretely that she may well not have thought of doing.

That little bit of a dangerous feeling excites women!

This can show them your confidence and create a strong bond between you.

Once she is happy to go anywhere with you, you have gained her trust.

She feels confident that you can make her feel the way she likes to feel.

Remember though that men and woman are different; they have different thought processes.

Keeping this fact in check assists in realising why your woman may behave in a non-logical manner at times, when least expected - without exactly understanding why, as men will never ever be able to do that!

Women can have numerous: hesitations, reasons, and worries why they should not sexually escalate.

Feelings of fear; consequences (like pregnancy); being taken advantage of; regrets later — all these can prevent her from acting spontaneously, which is all part of the natural way humans are designed.

After all, the women do most of the work in promulgating the species, the man does comparably nothing.

She has these in-built primal selective and security checks to consider (for want of better words) before committing to the act of a union with a man.

Generally speaking:

Men think in facts and *the NOW.*

Women think in flows and *the FUTURE.*

Keep the flirting experience with her going, this is like we were saying before; flick back a few steps into *Objective 2,* or even Obj*ective 1* momentarily.

The inexperienced, perhaps greedy type of man will rush into sex, which invariably just switches women off.

Bad and wrong move!

When she is at YOUR place, for say the first time, don't rush anything!

She needs to go through a process of feeling safe and secure in unfamiliar surroundings.

Her first visit is usually JUST for a cup of coffee and a chat.

It's all about her building trust in your and feeling secure with you.

Go slowly, with restraint even, maybe two steps forward and one step backwards.

Observe her responses!

Of course, every situation is different.

She may well have such a strong desire for you that all she wants to do is for you to get to your place so that she can be undressing you (perhaps you simultaneously undressing her) before you've managed to close your door.

But maybe that's something mainly seen in the movies?

You of course would have your values and motives about how you wish the relationship to progress too.

When you're getting to a stage where you think she's "ready" for you, don't get overexcited with your behaviour or conversation.

Keep the conversation sensible, keep your cool, offer a bit of subtle restraint, treat the whole process as positive, but not a big deal or issue.

Never, ever, mentally view, or even say to her, that she is **EASY.**

In fact, deprogram this word **EASY** from your permanent memory.

Never say it around women.

They do not like it - they loathe it!

No woman ever wishes to feel or be told that they are an easy lay.

At this stage, all going to plan (if that's the right terminology?) your woman will need to think, and feel that this guy - YOU:

- knows me and can turn me on physically and mentally.

- is not just a good friend or a perverted creep.

- wants to give me a really good experience.

- is interested in pleasing me.

- doesn't judge me.

- thinks I'm really special and different to other women.

- is really attracted to me.

We can accentuate her added desire for you, now that you know she really trusts you, by stimulating curiosity, without strong anxieties or doubts.

Keep your confidence up, physically and by using sensual dialogue with her. If she backs off, that's fine, just be patient and allow her to build her emotional connections; you're appreciating her current limitations – which she will recognise from you and respect.

Women do like men to make adventurous moves though, and they will respond positively to such advances, when they're ready. It excites them; it's what they're expecting. So don't be overly cautious at this point in the relationship; a little bit of risk-taking here is appropriate.

Do this with surprises; she doesn't know what's going to happen next.

It will create a feeling that she wants to follow you.

Again, keep in mind, to flick back to the more subtle and gentle behaviours and actions in *Objective 1* and *Objective 2,* especially if you see her behaviour closing off.

Respect her boundaries that she might be showing.

But you can be confident in everything you do now; making bold moves which with she'll probably be excited and intrigued.

Don't be the nice sort of guy that doesn't take any risks; her seeing you taking risks is a powerful thing – that little bit of danger element which sparks their primal instincts.

Keep the communication doors open – use words that tell her that you're there to have fun with her, and that you're here because she's unique.

She'll open up her own desires if she feels she can relieve any anxieties to you.

Maybe say to her: "Hey if you don't like something I do, then pinch my ear hard."

Maybe you'd like to tell her – "You're driving me crazy. It's all your fault that I feel so crazy about you - I'm under your spell."

As your relationship gets deeper, it can be difficult at times to correctly read her responses and to gauge the feedback she shows.

She may use subtle ways to steer conversation to a more non-sexual tone at times; maybe breaking eye contact and moving out of an intimacy area if you've suggested it.

Try and recognise when this is happening – and don't try and force the issue – don't try and drive things home.

This is the time to flick back to less direct approaches and non-sensual conversation.

She may need a bit more time, for herself, or a bit more courting in a non-sensuous way from you.

It's like a recalibrate or reconsolidate action - playing it cool on your part – so her desire is built up again. Listen to what she's saying and try and act accordingly to build her desire again.

A little trick could be to pull away from her when she may expect you to pull her to you; don't touch her; she'll wonder why.

Then a little later make physical intimacy by perhaps touching or hugging, it'll feel much more intense to her.

There are many other ways (use your imagination) for you to not carry out an anticipated behaviour, then do it a little later; the whole resultant feeling is amplified for her, and her desire will be intense.

Summary of the above objectives

Most women are sub-consciously tuned into these objectives and stages, as discussed above.

Men unfortunately are invariably not tuned in; hence the need for men to be more conscious, and better educated, to create a more mutual comfortable understanding with women.

Your behaviour and techniques will be different for each objective and phase, as outlined, depending on each situation.

You must wait and gauge a woman's reactions before moving onwards to subsequent stages of the relationship, knowing that it is normal to bounce back in the process at times if required.

So, in summary, we need to be confident as we show our intentions to form a relationship, by our body language and verbal cues, humour, and touch.

Using correct techniques, as discussed, we're able to establish an emotional connection, without telling our whole life story; by showing our vulnerabilities and strengths which will earn her trust in us.

She will have a deeper desire to find out more about you as your relationship becomes deeper.

Keep on surprising her and watch for her reactions.

PART 2

Managing and living with women

So now we've done all the fun hard work and we're established in our "happy" relationship.

Like everything in this world, relationships must be maintained.

The laws of nature dictate that nothing stays still; everything is in a constant change of flux.

Personal relationships are no exception; if we wish to keep our relationships healthy, we need to constantly be situationally aware of where we are, and have some form of idea where we're going, to keep our relationships healthy and clean.

Each situation is different; no two relationships are the same.

There are no hard and fast rules that apply to all relationships, only general guidelines.

Some general questions and answers to stimulate thinking with open-minded curiosity on the subject:

Is there a problem with women?

Know and confess; many men believe that women are problems.

Why?

They think differently, act differently.

Men and women are sired differently.

Why the differences?

Maybe you have thought, that ideally, there are no reasons for confusion or problems.

Feelings of guilt may prohibit your natural analysis of your relationship. Unnecessary stress can make the situation worse when it's not fully understood.

What is the extent of any confusion or problems in YOUR relationship?

Each relationship is different; no set hard and fast rules can be applied to every situation, but general guidelines do help. If you're fortunate to have a woman who is relatively comfortable to be with, and both your values towards life are similar, your problem may be quite small.

Some women enter relationships for future acquired affluence (Gold-diggers is the informal term often used here – women who dig for money).

Perhaps your woman is exploiting you for other reasons.

You will need to determine the extent, and basis, of anything that you're uncomfortable with in your relationship.

How long, do you think, you have felt uncomfortable?

This analogy is really part of number two above but deserves a separate mention.

In other words, how long has it been going on.

You may be surprised when you sit down and quietly think of your situation, the relationship, with your woman.

Can you alleviate your problem, your situation?

Be confident that you can.

All is not lost; do not be disheartened.

The following points provide some solutions to assist you to enhance balanced interdependence.

Does thinking like a woman help?

Women are always hunting!

That is, they are always watching and looking for suitable partners by varying degrees; it's their in-built breeding instinct.

Women have a total devotion to producing offspring.

Men invariably just want a sexual relationship.

Women do wish to form a relationship - a good, solid, stable, secure situation where she can raise her off-spring.

Women are not cold and hard to get, but they need to be taken through a procedural sequence (courtship) for her (and to a much lesser degree the man) to feel comfortable.

Because she does most of the work in producing offspring, she must be sure of her reasons to committing to her mate.

By using empathy, in thinking like a woman, you may approach some understanding of women.

Does analysing your own specific issues help?

Each person, each relationship, is different; only you can determine the factors and extent of your problem. You need to think of the factors within your own situation.

How long does confusion, or problems last?

The effort and work needed to live with women is not going to go away; it's part of life, part of our make-up.

We can only really mitigate it, reduce its intensity so it's manageable, within our relative comfort zones in our lives.

Is it just best to leave a relationship if it gets too complicated?

Again, every situation is different. Only you can decide if it is worth staying in your relationship.

Relationships invariably end because people's core values were perhaps not fully recognised at the start of a relationship, or one's personal values have changed to an unacceptable level or dimension, relative to the other person's values.

Men and women can change their core values as they journey through life, although it's rare.

Relationship breakdowns usually occur because these values weren't recognised and appreciated by couples during the initial relationship stages.

It's the amount and direction of these changes that are the main factors that determine whether a relationship will survive or not.

There usually is varying degrees of problems in relationships.

Some are major and perhaps not able to be resolved.

Some are not too serious and can be mollified to keep a relationship going on.

Some interesting clichés:

"Better the devil you know than the one you don't".

"The grass is not always greener on the other side of the hill".

"Life is not perfect".

Life's examples in numerous situations tend to show that it is sometimes better to stick with what you have than risk something unknown.

Only you can decide whether to maintain, repair, or leave your relationship, based on the characteristics that hold your relationship together.

Why is there a common trend after a period of approximately seven years,

(nicknamed: "the seven-year itch") when couples separate or divorce?

Most likely the couple had different values right from the start of their relationship that were tolerable, or maybe even ignored.

So, at the beginning of the relationship these differences were not an issue.

However, after a period, (seven years seems to be a common period, but it could be even twenty years) these differences in values may have amplified; may become a focus, and the relationship cannot continue.

A relationship split is inevitable.

A true story.

Years ago, a trusted elderly friend told me (I forget how the subject arose) that he'd never take a mistress – he just couldn't be bothered.

Being much younger, and in the prime of my manhood then, I was a bit confused, as to why, given the opportunity, and if there were no personal moral or religious grounds, any man wouldn't jump at the chance to enjoy physical sensual pleasure with another woman.

It was only when I matured in later years that I could appreciate the value of my friend's wisdom; I understood his reasons when I was in a similar situation.

I was able to make a wise choice.

I clearly recalled his words: "*One problem is enough.*"

Myth: Men with a harem of women are happy.

(One would most sincerely doubt it!)

Do we enjoy the challenges relationships present?

Yes, enjoy; challenges will always be here; they're not going away – ever!

It is an important part of life - as everything on our beautiful blue planet!

Once you have relationships criteria under some form of tolerable control, or in some managed format, you will enjoy what they have to offer.

Life would be boring without them.

SEDUCTIVE SECRETS

Imagine life with no problems to solve, no challenges or situations to keep us alert, satisfied and motivated.

It would be just too boring!

Be comfortable in your managed relationship situation.

Nothing great is easily won.

No Pain – No Gain

PART 3

Some of life's basics and general information

Living day-to-day in a comfortable and stable relationship situation ideally must be satisfactory for both genders.

Basic primal needs must be met – one of these basic needs is having sex.

Why mention this basic primal activity?

Because, in the "final analogy", or at the "end of the day" excuse the clichés, we are really just here to pass on our genes.

This is a primal instinct – to promulgate the species.

However, a woman needs to be (you can fill in the blank spaces – the one time a crude atrocious word will be used!) "f _ _ _ ed in the right way"; the way that she personally likes.

If her needs in this respect are not met, then she may naturally go and seek it somewhere else, perhaps reluctantly if she is subject to her personal values of strict social or religious rules.

But affairs do occur; always have done, and always will.

In decades gone by, most women (and men too) were virgins before they married.

Hence it was a huge risk for a desirable positive outcome of a sexually compatible relationship, to satisfy the needs of both the man and the woman, within the constitution of marriage.

One can only assess that probably more than half of these virginal marriages resulted in unhappy and unfulfilled women.

Women were invariably the gender that suffered.

Of course, nowadays, (over 99% would be an educated estimate) couples check each other out in most aspects, including sexual skills, before settling for a permanent relationship.

Nature does have a very useful playing card that it uses when it comes to relationships, not just for men/women relationships, but for any gender combination of friendship or intimate relationships.

There is always a chemistry of varying degrees between all people.

Notice how you "get-on" with some people, but not so well with others.

You may feel very uncomfortable when in close proximity with some people!

Chemistry between people – males and females included – is the unexplained.

Perhaps chemistry is Divine – and you can interpret the word Divine anyway you wish, depending on your personal philosophical and spiritual beliefs.

Many people believe that when meeting others where a natural chemistry and rapport is established, there exists evidence of past lives – in another time.

Again, you may interpret that according to your own personal beliefs.

Like friendship relationships with men – some you get on with – others you're not too comfortable with - in working, leisure or sport activities, the same scenario applies to women.

Example of the use of Natural Chemistry

In the United Kingdom, during the Second World War, after RAF bomber crews had completed their training, they were all assembled in their training batch, which may have consisted of perhaps over two hundred men. They were then simply asked to sort themselves out into crews; for example, some aircraft may have had several distinct roles, pilot, navigator, air-gunner, etc.

Invariably, it was later determined that the men who readily allotted themselves into a complete aircraft crew performed the best, and perhaps even survived longer. This was an example of applying human chemistry for the maximum gain.

The ones who didn't readily strike a rapport with others, and establish common ground had to be systematically placed in crews to make up the missing allocations and numbers. They unfortunately didn't get to choose their fellow crew members.

Miscellaneous TIT - BITS

When meeting women

- eye contact

- upright body language

- try and be the first to talk - use humour with a joke

- a good tone in your voice; it's *how* we say things, not *what* we say

- try coming in on a high note, making a dramatic impression with your words; sensational perhaps – if the situation feels right; maybe a compliment specific to her; talk about high passion topics – positive emotion

- take up space.

- TOUCH – a short early non-sexual touch; measure her feedback and response

- tease in a playful way – in moderation

- tell stories but don't rush; be animated with expressions; teaser curiosity style in moderation; compliment her

- be prepared and willing to laugh at yourself

- repeat her name

- make her laugh (humour)

- engage her friends

- ask her to do something for you

- wear red or black

Once you have developed a conversation and rapport with her, listen to what she's saying; if you feel you've run out of things to say then that is an indication that you are not in the moment.

Remember

- have unconditional trust in yourself in what you say and do.

- there are unlimited opportunities out there because there are unlimited women.

- don't try to act or create a fake impression; show your natural expressions and actions; show her who you are.

- create interest – power presence – you're special.

- recognise chemistry – flirt.

- build up some mystery about yourself; provide information about yourself but leave gaps by not overdoing it.

- make yourself scarce occasionally, limit your interactions with her; become less available.

Being a confident man

- trust yourself

- uninhibited – no fear

- don't try to impress anyone

- impose personal boundaries

- feel entitled to positive treatment

When around women

- act just like you're around your friends; you're not a fake or are putting on a big act

- do not think, at any time, to put on the *big act*, to put on a show for women by showing them how big and great you are; it's the WRONG behaviour

- women will pick up any silly false acts immediately

- women, by their natural in-built primal instincts, read faces and attitudes on *autopilot*; they sense your behaviour without having to think about it

- be comforted in the fact though that when feeling nervous, or slightly out of your comfort zone, in certain situations, it is good to honestly admit to her how you feel

- women interpret honesty in a man who faces up to his fears, and it will fire up their primal instincts as a positive sign with you.

Touch – remember

- women like to be touched – by people and men they feel comfortable with

- don't be afraid or unduly hesitate to touch in non-sensual places

- initially, touch in a safe area or zone which tests her response, like her shoulder, wrist, or lower arm; don't wait too long, and don't over touch her

Types of touch

- casual

- shielding (guarding)

- romantic - like holding hands or stroking her hair

- sexual intimacy touches

Speaking

- it's not *what* we say but *how* we say it, in terms of presence, intention, and character

- when engaging conversation with women, don't look or seek logical solutions

- women just need to talk; most just like to waffle and gossip

- women's speaking behavioural patterns makes them feel comfortable and secure

- achieving a speaking outlet with you means that you're on the way to

gaining an inner trust from a woman

Women's indications that they like and are "into" you

- quiet and attentive with you

- acts helpless

- teases you

- laughs at all your jokes

- constantly fixing herself, especially her hair

- appears nervous

- maybe denies liking you, but in reality she does

Some false biases and myths

Men consider a women's looks to be the main attraction.

Men consider that their own looks are not good.

The reality is that women focus on attention and appreciation as the main attraction trait to men – looks are not the main factor that they single out.

If a man sees a relatively physically attractive woman, he may fool himself into thinking that the woman is of a high status and may try to offer or produce favours for this "attractive" woman.

The reality is that women see through all this, by their strong intuitive skills, and find these favours repulsive.

Men may find themselves with insecurity flaws, thinking bad and negative thoughts, and assuming the worst, like they're never going to get a woman; there is a strong expectation of consistently losing.

If you think you'll lose, subconsciously, then you will behave accordingly.

Don't take women on FACE Value – do your own checking and use what little intuition that you have as a man.

Women can and do lie, in the game of love (and lust).

They can be - like men too – idealists and perfectionists.

Her first words may not be what she may wish to mean, in a manner of speaking; *EXCEPT the word NO.*

When a woman says NO – take that meaning as a literate **definite NO!!**

Women's three main primal emotions

- Their *need to feel safe* – meaning you're no threat to her.

- Their *need to feel very special*, not just in what you say; they like to see they are different and appreciated by you.

- Their *need to feel sexy*; she needs you to notice and want her.

Try and show that you're selective with options; they want to see that you are

selective with available options, that is, when other women are around.

You've selected her!

Green flags that you're getting on well with a particular woman

Note – be aware though that your judgment in this area may get cluttered at times. She:

- gets your sense of humour

- is kind

- communicates during conflicts

- gets along with your friends

- she's close with her friends

- is supportive with you

- appears to you to be smart

- has her own interests

Stimulants

A colleague of mine once told me how he seemed to fail in women relationships and situations when he was a younger man, during his infant stage of picking up women. He explained how he thought that it was cool to take his date out and behave like he usually did when going out on the night socially with his mates. He'd have a few drinks, and a few more, enjoying himself, until usually towards the end of the evening, he'd feel a bit tired, perhaps even bored, and content, (obviously from the depressive effects of alcohol or drugs). This would transpire to his body language, and be picked up quickly by women, which would be an immediate turn off, to say the least.

What was my colleague doing wrong, in his younger, mad days?

Either he was very unaware of courting skills, or his behaviour was the result of a combination of drugs, alcohol, and partying.

Sure, he could have had a couple of drinks maybe and enjoyed the evening, but there comes a limit to what the human body can accept in terms of stimulants. Too many stimulants and the human body starts switching off, winding down to a sleepy and tired feeling. It's not just alcohol, but any form of partying, hard stimulant, or drug.

It can be good to remember some clever words, by alliteration, beginning with "B" when around women:

No:

- booze

- bragging

- boasting

- bullying

- bashfulness

- begging

Women can reduce a man's general awareness

Women can, in most situations, produce a false sense of security, and sometimes over-confidence in men. These undesirable attributes in some rare situations can be dangerous.

Perhaps the best example is military environments in combatant roles.

It is the male gender that has usually been tasked with defending the home, the country, (and the women).

However, in centuries gone by, over the course of countless wars, it has been recorded that women have helped men defend their lands and homes.

In recent modern times, World War I and World War II provided examples of women involved in active combatant roles, in some of the war theatres.

No accurate documented analysis, or statistics, of casualty numbers are readily available, even from these two recent two World Wars.

But since the late 1940's, in the enduring Middle East conflicts between Israel and neighboring Arab States, where Israeli women were actively involved in combatant roles alongside men, accurate casualty statistics have been recorded.

It has been determined, and recorded, that casualty rates in the Israeli forces were higher when women were fighting alongside men.

Why?

A man's primal instinct is to look out for and care for women.

In life and death situations (like active combat) a man's awareness is highly likely to be distracted by looking out for women's welfare.

This destroys the special bonds that exist between military men, the strict team unit, which is vital for their survival in combat situations.

They have been trained to rely on each other in life and death situations.

Also, compounded by this scenario, by placing a small number of women in a group of men, the men naturally (sub-consciously) compete – even fight - for the right to mate the women.

These primal instincts that govern our behavior and attitudes cannot be trained out of humans, as has been sometimes stated or assumed.

Approximately four decades ago, when women were generally allowed, and accepted into combatant military roles, the above reasoning and negative consequences were clearly reported and stated, to relevant government leaders, by senior professional military and civilian analysts at the time.

Their reports fell on deaf political ears.

In the past, some professional sporting teams have restricted their players access to women, some days before a major game. Reasons would no doubt include keeping the players' motivation and physical energy levels high.

However, I believe in recent times, the emotional advantages of having one's "woman" close by during times of high stress may have overridden old fashioned coach's rules!

Women can, depending on the distinct situation, be a frustrating distraction.

Conflicts

During the course of a developing relationship, conflicts invariably arise, it's part of life. In fact, a marriage or a partnership needs regular conflict to survive.

How best to comfortably handle it?

Have weekly meetings – call them SOS meetings.

Let them be soul-orientated, providing as much detail and feelings for both couple and partners.

Learn to communicate – whatever that takes.

Older men

Woman, generally, like older men because they usually are:

- not needy (or greedy)

- not over reactive – they are more stable under pressure

- competent with relationships - know how to have fun and be a leader

Women do like and often seek experienced men.

SIX SEXY things women crave in bedrooms

- foreplay

- your leadership, commands, and directions

- your physical dominance

- your appreciation, by telling her that you're having a great time and how good it all feels.

- oral and finger actions

- your full presence of being there – which also is an awareness of her feedback.

Informal relationship technical terms

Main key pick-up skills

Cool, calm, confident.

Visualise

What is your type? Examples: blonde; blue-eyed; tall; dark; black hair, and so forth.

Trust your instincts

Basic human chemistry.

Courtship

Women want it – men invariably don't see the point of it - but is a vital part of the arousal process for women – "wine and dining" women before bedding them.

Intuition

Women's is far, far, stronger than men's – they invariably know when they have found the "right" mate; the "one".

They do most of the work for re-production, so they need to know that they've chosen wisely for their own comforts and multiplication of the species.

It's an in-built basic primal instinct that they have.

It's like sharks when swimming or diving the depths of the sea; they'll usually see you before you see them.

Women learn this intuition naturally as children; by the time they reach late teenage years and adulthood they are on autopilot when figuring out if a man is someone that they wish to explore more with a view to copulate with.

Perfect

There is not the perfect woman out there; never has been and never will be.

Besides it's better the devil you know than the one you don't.

It is not a perfect world – accept that.

It is relatively common to see spinsters; these women can quite often have a false attitude of a perfect world – these women usually never marry or form intimate relationships.

Some men too, remain bachelors all their lives; some are just never able, or wanting to, click onto the wavelength of relating to women in an intimate way.

Relationship maintenance

Everything in this world must be maintained – everything!

Relationships are no exception, no matter how many years one has been in one.

Keep the ball rolling, don't stop being aware of your relationship.

There is a parable: put a stone in a jar during the first year of your marriage/partnership every time that you have had sex.

During the second year, take a stone out every time you have sex.

See if you can empty the jar over the course of the second year!

Nourish twilight years of your relationship.

People become more spiritual; there is always something new to find about your wife/partner.

Finding the Right Mate

Qualities to look for in studying a potential lifetime mate:

- easy to get on with

- shows interdependence qualities

- easy to communicate with

- same values

Outlook:

- settle permanently

- continually travel (drift)

- children

Take time out periodically

- give yourself breathing space at some stage of the courting process

- couples married for years will take time for themselves to reassess their situation, then come back together

Have a pre-matrimonial agreement which invariably may incorporate a TRUST arrangement, especially if large assets are at stake. Many unfortunate people in long term relationships have been caught in legal proceedings that follow breakups by having their respective original valuable assets squandered.

Do not have absolute faith in your emotions - they can ruin your original intentions if legal devices and procedures are not set up in place in the early stages of a relationship or marriage once couples make their commitments to each other.

Speed

Women – slow approach; slow procedures

Men – can be instantaneous; right now!

Thus, a man must learn the skill of a general procedural type of approach (courting) required to seduce and win a woman.

If these skills and techniques are not there, then the man will probably have difficulty in establishing a compatible relationship with a woman.

Rejection

ACCEPT rejection – after all, it's part of life in all facets of work and play.

Maybe, when you find yourself in this situation which you can't logically answer yourself why a woman is behaving as such, it could be the natural period of rejection for her, which women all have at certain times due to their hormone cycles.

SEDUCTIVE SECRETS

Over-reacting

Don't overdo any objectives or stages described in this book – feel the right time to back-off temporarily.

Orgasms

Women do not always automatically have or need orgasms; it depends on their menstrual cycle and emotional state at the time. They may still strongly desire sex but may not experience full pleasure or climax.

Men invariably, always have orgasms and complete their duty in delivering the seed, required for reproduction, to the woman.

Talking

- women do like to talk

- women LOVE talking

- talking helps women maintain their sense of security and well-being

- when you're talking to women, don't seek logical, decisive, factual answers or serious solutions to the world's problems

- women don't want or need logical or factual solutions

- women just love to talk light-heartedly; they love it

The Pickup

Invariably it's men who are left to do this task.

Women expect it - or most of them anyway.

It can be looked on as a measure of a man's worth to entice, woo, court the woman into a relationship, to a mating situation to reproduce.

She can gauge how good this "man" is by his skills in seducing her.

Responsible and normal women are no "walk-overs".

It's in their primate ancestral animal instincts to check-out potential mates to get the best seed to fertilise their eggs so they may spawn the best offspring.

It's something women have little control over, it's bred into their female human architecture.

Some salient similarities and facts

Life is essentially a competition – sperm compete to fertilise eggs.

Life is about learning new things – no pain means no gain.

Striving to succeed can entice one to feel alive.

People who wish for a total pleasurable life, in their work *and* play, are intoxicated in an unrealistic type of living zone.

They invariably have a breakdown at some point.

Happiness means striking a balance of striving, achieving, and accepting being a loser sometimes.

The challenge can be much against yourself to push boundaries, though we are also competing against other people.

Men courting women is no exception in the game of life.

Of course, sometimes, though its rather rare, women do step out of their nominal role and become the hunter.

They strongly see or intuitively feel a certain man is for them, so they go out of their normal role and zone to entice the man to form a relationship.

Done with a positive and fun like attitude, the act of courtship is enlightening and pleasurable, like most things in life.

Indeed, life in general is a challenge, and courting a woman to bed her and to form a long-lasting relationship is no exception.

Without challenges, humans quickly become dormant, demotivated, and listless, perhaps even depressed.

<u>Supplication</u>

This means doing things for a woman to make her want to feel something for you (favours for feelings).

This is not an area you want to delve into or seek.

Women will lose respect for you once they pick up your attitude and approach if you're exhibiting this behaviour.

So, periodically, check that your actions are *NOT SUPPLICATING*, that is, doing something for her approval.

Lookers

Interpret this any way you think or believe – it is a general statement written in simple language and terms.

This is a sweeping generalisation, but invariably many men have expressed their opinion that it does have a fair amount of truth when one says:

Women who are "Good Lookers" usually have an unbalanced, basically immature attitude.

Why?

Who knows?

Perhaps these unfortunate women are conditioned by social ego, at an early age, and other games played in society, and this unnatural condition becomes firmly established and engrained in their attitude.

They may be a good "lay" in bed initially, and maybe for some period, but when it comes to the other required attributes of life and living, generally most "good lookers" just don't have the basic life skills and/or the required balanced attitude that a happy, fulfilled life requires.

Perhaps these women just desire continuous pure pleasure – which is of course a non-reality.

Life requires a balance of work, suffering, and pleasure.

However, you might be lucky to find one with good looks, a sensible attitude and the most essential for a peaceful balanced life – common sense.

That is the Achilles heel of a sustained happy relationship with any woman – a woman (and a man!) that both have plenty of *common sense.*

Celebrities are good examples of failed relationships; we hear about them more, because they're invariably constantly in the media.

Usually, they get together in a relationship before determining if each other's deep core values are the same, or at least similar. Invariably, impulsive basic physical desires, based on sexual forces, bring these people together, a union which is enhanced by their working and leisure life-styled environments. As they go through life, sometimes a catalyst, an event, or other issues cause these values to be examined and focused.

If each person's blueprint of their own values is not mirrored by the other person, then the relationship will have friction, which if sufficiently severe, can lead to the relationship dissolving.

This, of course, can and does happen to many relationships – not just the so-called famous, and celebrities.

Don't be put off by Good Lookers.

They know who they are, and they know how most men react to them.

These women invariably feel and think they have a lot of control over most men, because of their so-called "beauty power".

It's a false ego and false pretence that will never go away so long as we're human beings.

But these types of women can be levelled out to a balanced plane using clever dialogue.

This approach has been called names such as: negative talk; put-downs, etc. It is not intended to insult the "Looker" woman, but to simply humanise them, to let them know that you think they're just an ordinary human being and normal everyday woman.

What does a man say to approach and break the ice to get a rapport going with such women?

One obvious way is to look at what they're wearing, or how they're dressed, and say something noncomplimentary but constructive like:

"Your long blonde hair keeps impeding your vision when it's windy, but you can simply tie it back if you like, so it's better to control."

"Those high heels look like a great style, but they can get caught on these uneven cobblestones if you're not walking carefully."

Say anything that isn't pleasingly positive but is negative and provides an answer or alternative for her. Then most likely, she'll respond in a neutral human way; she knows you're not trying to blatantly pick her up, and a general rapport could be established.

It may lead on from there if you so desire.

<u>Harems</u>

What to say about Harems?

The word can raise notions of ancient civilisations where a king had scores of wives, kept in captivity, but usually well looked after, and at his leisure, he selected any for his pleasure.

The king would invariably know when a particular woman was responsive to his approaches or desires, as they would probably be at the point in their menstrual cycle for mating, when they strongly desired sex.

They may have felt privileged to be part of the king's select group of women and were happy to spawn his off-spring.

Ancient civilisations in such places as Africa and Asia were noted for such aristocratic social structures; however, some Western religious sects of recent decades were reported to espouse Harem type behaviours.

In modern times, some celebrities, notably modern musicians, could be accused of similar behaviours that depict a Harem type of structure. No names stated, but some celebrities have been known to have many wives/partners and children with multiple women – an indirect form of a miniature ancient harem.

These celebrities can be described as seeking doses of pleasure, to their naive detriment. They would not experience a true intimate lifelong relationship.

One may often think that it must be great to have more than one woman, like a mistress or having a secret lover, an affair.

However, generally speaking, in all consideration, one "problem" is usually enough, so a notable (anon) wise old man once said.

Reverse Roles

Sometimes, when you least expect it, the roles of the man/woman; hunter/hunted can be reversed.

It's not always one-way.

The laws of nature, as discussed, are that a man invariably hunts and endeavours to persuade a woman that he's a good mate for her.

However, sometimes, a woman may show or act in a way that's beyond what you'd expect their anticipated or natural reactions would be, whether they be from your advances, techniques and courting or just from what you may think is not normal behaviour.

Indeed, one could say it's maybe not the natural behaviour expected of women who are tuned into being courted and wooed – but that's OK – we can go with it.

It may be a pleasant surprise.

Remember we are all in a glass house; you will be watching her, for her reactions from your verbal and body language; but be assured **that she has been also watching you too,** closer than what you may have thought!

Women are always looking for "that mate".

How motivated, and how hard they are looking, depends on numerous factors such as their situation, age, and various other circumstances.

Usually after a relatively substantive period of courting, when a woman has had ample times to watch you, observe your behaviour, listen to what you say (and *HOW* you're saying things!) she may come to a concrete conclusion that you are the man for her, and that she really does want to get laid by you!

Sometimes, this is a decision taken by a woman in unexpected times, in various forms, when maybe she, and you of course, least expect it.

The signs and signals can be subtle, sensitive, maybe camouflaged, or conversely, perhaps quite blatant, and direct.

The following are real-life examples, which I experienced, relating to women's interests and behaviour. You probably have examples from your own experiences that you are able to relate to.

Example

A few decades ago, I was a guitar player in a club band. There was this particular lady whom I knew relatively well as a friend; we were good acquaintances.

I was a bit naïve in those days, and quite slow in interpreting women's signs when I was young.

One night when our band had taken a break between sets at the club, I found her sitting on the stage close to my specific guitar speaker, with a couple of her friends, that I hadn't seen before. Her behaviour was blatantly obvious, especially as she kept looking at me as our band members came back on stage, but I didn't cue into it. I had ignored her positive signs that she wanted to get to know me better.

Example

At a lake holiday resort, a type of back packers' place, in the shared dining room, a lovely young lady just sat down in front of me across the table and started casually eating her meal. There were plenty of other vacant seats, but she chose to sit directly opposite me. She can't have seen me for very long, during that particular day, after I had arrived.

I was only staying there a day or two, but for her it was obvious that she wanted to (very quickly!) get to know me. I was too occupied with other things going on and with other distractions, so I didn't exploit the situation.

(Silly me!)

The lesson here is to keep awareness about you for women's signs, and use them to your advantage, if you wish to.

Example

I had belonged to a cosmopolitan type of club for quite a few months, which had a quiet little bar where people would mix and mingle socially as they do.

A particular lady, whom I knew mainly by sight confronted me once. We may have had some previous minor conversations, but essentially, we only knew each other as mutual club members, by sight.

One day this attractive lady and I were standing at the bar, in proximity getting our respective drinks, when she, quite clearly, and unemotionally, politely addressed me stating: "That she would like to discretely screw me."

(Can't be more direct than that can we?)

It's amazing how a woman can just create a general calmness and establish a level plane of honesty. This lady did this to me, as we chatted about how she'd like me to "bed" her, with other people mingling around the bar, just out of earshot – thankfully!

Examples of situations that are not uncommon

Perhaps you may be entertaining a woman in your home or apartment, and find that she's wandered off somewhere, whilst you were briefly pre-occupied – maybe whilst you were cooking that lovely dinner you promised her!

You discover that she's found your "man-bed" and is curled up naked between the sheets, smiling, perhaps saying to you not to hurry, as we have all night!

She's been waiting for you to find her. Dinner may have to wait – be sure to switch the oven off!

If this situation is what you deeply desire and want, then go for it, but keep your cool, maintain a slow approach and don't overreact.

Enjoy, and make it good for her! Don't go too fast with your immediate actions; she's probably still a bit nervous and not fully aroused.

Be the sensuous gentleman and slowly stoke her to full arousal with your expert stimulation and control.

Make it very, very special; she won't forget this first experience with you, and she'll no doubt love you for it.

Conversely of course, you may find your woman starts stroking you all over - very assertively – perhaps even trying to rip your clothes off aggressively, as soon as you've walked through the door and shut it in your, or her, place.

She's obviously very aroused and wants you without any undue waiting, but again, keep your cool a bit. "Steady as she goes," as they say on the high seas!

Dating

A quick look at this traditional term – and some other related information - when a man and a woman go out together.

Dating is one form of courting. Dating terminology isn't used much nowadays.

It's usually accepted that if a man and woman, the first time, or initially that they get together, are going to a common place, on a set day and time, then it's an automatic date.

No formal request, usually by the man, must be made; no initial meeting of parents or guardians when picking the woman up from her place of abode, or home, before going out on "the date". We invariably don't refer to it as a date anymore.

But in the initial stages of establishing a relationship, during the courting process, there are similarities experienced that are true just as there were in the past when dating was seen to be the official first stages of getting to know the other gender, of determining if one felt like establishing a serious relationship with a person, with the long-term view of marriage and commitment.

Treat this dating topic as a guide if you have that goal of seeking a long term committed relationship. It's not to be used as an introduction for one-night stands of a quick fling in bed with the prettiest ladies whilst in their local town.

Having a goal of finding a long-term relationship with a woman involves setting guidelines and behavioural disciplines.

Ask yourself: Who are you? What type of person are you? What are your core values and principles?

These deep questions may not be readily answered; it will depend on how much you've thought about yourself and what your life goals are. But having a general idea of where you are in the world, and what you want, will provide a good grounding when meeting new people and women and establishing relationships.

What type of person will complement your values, and your long-term goals? Does that person have the attributes that you seek?

Some people come from many failed relationships; they perhaps enjoy not achieving their goals or succeeding; they may be constant moaners, wounded from their past; victims of love, is a phrase often used.

They repeat their behavioural patterns without going forward; are maybe addicted to love; not giving themselves time to grow; making same mistakes; happy in their own grief or self-pity.

It may be difficult to recognise such people, but one's own intuition usually is a good tool and guide.

One can't make a cake out of sour cream (excuse the cliché)

Chemistry between people (as previously discussed) becomes readily apparent when you're within a few feet of someone, gazing and talking, a little touching and usually finding that your behaviours are mirrored or synced.

Dating is awkward – it is a form of seeking ritual.

The more you expose yourself as a seeker, the higher the likelihood of a positive result.

Feeling good about yourself will entice people to want to be with you.

Attention by smiling, saying positive things, a mutual interest; creating desire around why you're worth getting to know with natural actions achieves results.

ASKING for a date creates vulnerability – as we naturally don't desire rejection, that is a "no" answer. However, nothing great is easily won, and a small risk or gamble is required to find out if a date is going to happen. One must ask!

Rejection is a fact of life, and most rejection from dating and relationships is because of misinterpretation.

Positive communication creates intimate connections, listening more than talking, without interrupting, complaining, or discussing past relationships.

Mutual interests enable common ground to build on.

Sometimes, after a relationship has built to an intimate phase (like sex) one or both parties may back off or retreat, creating a feeling of rejection.

It's a natural part of behavioural traits; communication is important at this stage to keep the relationship going if desired.

Rituals of courtship do take time.

Some people develop a workaholic approach to life, so they escape the need to build their emotional life. They feel that they: need to stay busy; control everything; be perfect; feel that they don't deserve success; and they don't like any form of rejection.

A balanced life of establishing separate work and play criteria will provide a romantic revival.

Breaking relationships (being single again) can enable personal growth, and fresh self-awareness.

It can be difficult, especially to make changes within yourself that you may desire.

Take time before committing to a new romance. Rushing straight back into a relationship is a rebound to fill an emptiness inside which probably won't fulfil your needs.

With single parents, you're effectively dating the children too. A slow pace in the relationships is essential, making the children feel important too. Don't get involved with support partners problems.

Stepparents are never real parents; it can take years for children to fully accept stepparents.

Courtship rules have changed; it's not as straightforward as previous decades where there were set rules and most people abided by them.

There's no real honour in staying single; don't wait for proper introductions.

Meet as many people as you can.

Don't expect connections to be simple; take a risk; risk is part of romance.

Sex doesn't compensate for romance.

Women love honest communication – fewer facts and more personal views and outlooks.

If you think your behaviour needs changing, then do it – your heart will follow; action, then emotion.

Not every date leads to a relationship.

Smile even if you don't feel like it!

Women's Reading

Here it is – the final part of this *MAN* book – especially for you ladies that have read through so far, for your own curiosity and stimulation.

These points I'm sure will assist you in your own quest for pleasure and fulfilment, whatever that personally means to you!

For the men, it's a bonus and interesting sort of read.

I trust this assists any women who would like to enhance their relationship with their male partner/husband.

Some of these points provide very old attributes, that go back hundreds of years, that are at the core of any relationship.

The power you possess

As a woman, you do have an underlying power over men.

You may not fully understand or appreciate this God-given (excuse the cliché) attribute – but you have it in you.

Don't abuse it because if you do, at some later stage in your life, it will backfire on you and likely harm you.

Use your power wisely.

Your man is not a slave

Much literature has been written on this issue over the decades.

Some women find it humorous to refer to their male counterparts as just working slaves for their own pleasure.

No doubt some men enjoy, or are happy with their relationship, or situation being in a Master/Slave situation.

Perhaps men have a low self-esteem or confidence and are unable to break out of that role.

Whatever you own personal situation or aspirations in your relationship and life, if you dwell on, or abuse, a Master/Slave situation, you will do so at your future peril.

Trust your intuition in selecting a mate

As a woman you have been blessed with more intuition, or inner knowing, than your fellow menfolk.

As the gender that does most (if not all) of the work to reproduce our species, biological makeup and evolution has provided women with this trait to assist with the on-going well-being and propagation of our species.

Your deep-rooted, ingrained intuition will not fail you.

Feel it.

Trust it.

Obey it.

Most women "know" when they have met their true "mate".

Endeavour to always dress well

No doubt easier said than done for a lot of women regarding their occupations, but men do notice (the majority anyway) and appreciate women looking beautiful in their own individual characteristic right.

Dress can be difficult when one's job dictates the specific attire needed for work or activities, but where possible dress accordingly.

Give confidence

Admittedly we all need confidence, of varying amounts, at certain phases of our lives.

Women, generally being more mature, by age, than men are ahead in this facet. Hence, men invariably require more nudging along with confidence in their daily lives.

A man's partner/wife is an ideal avenue to provide this assistance through life.

Don't neglect your manners

Say please.

Say thank-you.

Men love it, especially as a prelude respectively before and after sex.

These simple words said at the appropriates times may bond your man to you like super-glue!

Men do expel a lot of energy to fulfil the sexual act, depending on their age and current physical state.

Sex

Enjoy it.

Most women usually have more knowledge in this subject than the average male.

So, encouragement, and teaching may be needed for your ultimate pleasure.

Don't assume that your man knows it all and that it's his duty to provide all the foreplay and answers for great sex.

You can play an active part too if you so desire.

Physical and mental abuse

If your partner or husband ever physically hits or strikes you, then it is time to leave.

They have lost respect for you.

Go.

Get out of the situation.

Don't go back to the relationship.

This is a very emotional issue as most women perhaps don't wish to admit that their partner is abusing them, or perhaps think that they have no other options or any place to go to get out of their situation.

Complications obviously arise when children are involved.

There are *always* options for anyone in *any* situation.

If you have no immediate avenues of assistance from relatives or friends, there are usually government authorities and agencies to assist people who are being abused.

Contact them and explain your situation.

ADDED BONUS
Tips for Woman

<u>Enhancing sexual pleasure from your man</u>

Say his first name often.

Say please (before) and thank-you (after) – good manners – he'll respect you immensely!

"Blow jobs" (we all know what they are!) work wonders; a man will fly to the moon for you when given a sensuous blow-job.

Tell him how "big" he his.

A sensuous smile and saying how you enjoyed all of it.

Suck his nipples, ears.

Playing with his penis, by manoeuvring yourself so it plays all over your body, especially your breasts; this is stimulating for you and for him.

Kissing – lots of tongue play – right into his mouth exploring every cavity.

Ask him if you may please play with him.

Give vocal groans and responses, it'll bring him (and probably you) on and make him feel good.

Being secured during sexual endeavours

Experienced and mature sexual women sometimes feel the inclination to be tied up when being made love to.

Blatantly asking your man to do this may scare him away from the task - perhaps even permanently!

Having your man tie you up, or secure you to the bed, requires a delicate approach.

Gentle and very subtle words are required so as not to create negative thoughts in your man. It can be a psychological barrier to a man to physically secure a woman.

Only you can determine what, how and when to ask your man these intimate requests. Perhaps by dropping the hint by having pieces of rope or cloth conveniently placed near the bed is sufficient for him to see the signs and complete the task.

Practical suggestions would be to have securing rope or cloth just loosely tied around arms or palms of your hands so that you can release yourself at any time at your own free will.

Other parts of the body are not so important, but it is better to be able to release your hands by yourself. Obviously, hand-cuffs and the like, often seen in sex-shops, are not suitable in this respect.

Why?

Read this (true!) interesting story:

Years ago, a man tied his sexual partner on their bed, very securely.

He then changed into a costume he's bought from a sex shop – a crotch-less Batman suit!

Thinking he could fly like batman does in the movies, he climbed on top of a wardrobe and leaped off, intending to land on the bed to exploit his sexual appetite.

However, he landed short and fell onto the floor, breaking his back – literally.

Unable to move, and with his partner securely tied up, the couple remained in their respective positions for about two days before they were eventually found and rescued.

The moral of the story?

"Don't go overboard."

END

About the Author

Roger Rickard lives in the Wakatipu region of New Zealand. Feeling at home amongst the mountains and lakes, his outdoor spirit encompasses many sports and activities.

With professional disciplines in aviation he's extensively travelled to many regions in the world. Bring passionate about music, having written and recorded some of his material in the pop/folk genre, he enjoys playing solo acoustic guitar and in musical groups.

Roger felt that a self help book on heterosexual relationships, and how to achieve them, would benefit many.

More books along similar lines could be on the way!

Roger admits that he's not an expert on women!

Who is?

Any comments on the book are welcomed at: penspublishingtrading@gmail.com

Milton Keynes UK
Ingram Content Group UK Ltd.
UKHW020625291123
433416UK00016B/1052